SPACE VOYAGE

THE UNIVERSE AND ITS MYSTERIES

CATHERINE BARR

PowerKiDS press

Published in 2022 by The Rosen Publishing Group, Inc.
29 East 21st Street, New York, NY 10010

Originally Published in English by Haynes Publishing under the title: Space Pocket Manual © Catherine Barr 2019

All rights reserved. No part of this book may be reproduced in any form without permission in writing from the publisher, except by a reviewer.

Cataloging-in-Publication Data

Names: Barr, Catherine.
Title: The universe and its mysteries / Catherine Barr.
Description: New York : PowerKids Press, 2022. | Series: Space voyage
Identifiers: ISBN 9781725331914 (pbk.) | ISBN 9781725331938 (library bound) | ISBN 9781725331921 (6 pack) | ISBN 9781725331945 (ebook)
Subjects: LCSH: Cosmology--Juvenile literature. | Astronomy--Juvenile literature.
Classification: LCC QB983.B365 2022 | DDC 520--dc23

Design and layout by Richard Parsons

Photo Credits: Cover, p. 1 (control panel) Sky vectors/shutterstock.com; cover, p. 1 (background) Vadim Sadovski/Shutterstock.com; pp. 6-32 (background), 3, 4-5, 7, 8, 11 (left), 12-13 (bottom), 14 (bottom), 15 (both), 18, 19, 20 (both), 21 (both), 23, 26; pp. 6, 10, 11 (right), 13 (both), 22 (both), 24 (all), 25 Courtesy of NASA; p. 9 https://commons.wikimedia.org/wiki/File:Einstein_1921_by_F_Schmutzer_-_restoration.jpg; p. 14 (top), 16 (bottom), 17 (bottom), 28 (top), 29 (top) Alamy; p. 16 (top) https://commons.wikimedia.org/wiki/File:R%C3%B8mer,_Ole_(ur_Ber%C3%B8mte_danske_maend).jpg; p. 17 (top) Getty Images; p. 27 (top) https://commons.wikimedia.org/wiki/File:The_Sounds_of_Earth_-_GPN-2000-001976.jpg; p. 27 (bottom) https://commons.wikimedia.org/wiki/File:Voyager_Golden_Record_fx.png; p. 28 (bottom) https://commons.wikimedia.org/wiki/File:Arthur_C._Clarke_1965.jpg; p. 29 (bottom) https://commons.wikimedia.org/wiki/File:Stephen_Hawking.StarChild.jpg.

Manufactured in the United States of America

CPSIA Compliance Information: Batch #CSPK22. For Further Information contact Rosen Publishing, New York, New York at 1-800-237-9932.

CONTENTS

THE BIG BANG.. 4

A QUIET BEGINNING.................................. 6

SPACETIME 8

FORCES OF NATURE 10

LIGHT IN SPACE 12

WILL IT ALL END?.................................... 14

SCIENTISTS.. 16

IN THE DARK 18

WORMHOLES 20

LOOKING FOR LIFE.................................. 22

FOCUS ON ALIEN LIFE 24

ALIEN NOISES 26

DISCOVERERS 28

GLOSSARY 30

FOR MORE INFORMATION 31

INDEX 32

THE BIG BANG

Space and time started with a Big Bang. Nobody knows if anything existed before the Big Bang or what triggered this massive cosmic explosion. What we do know is that this split second when the universe began happened about 13.8 billion years ago.

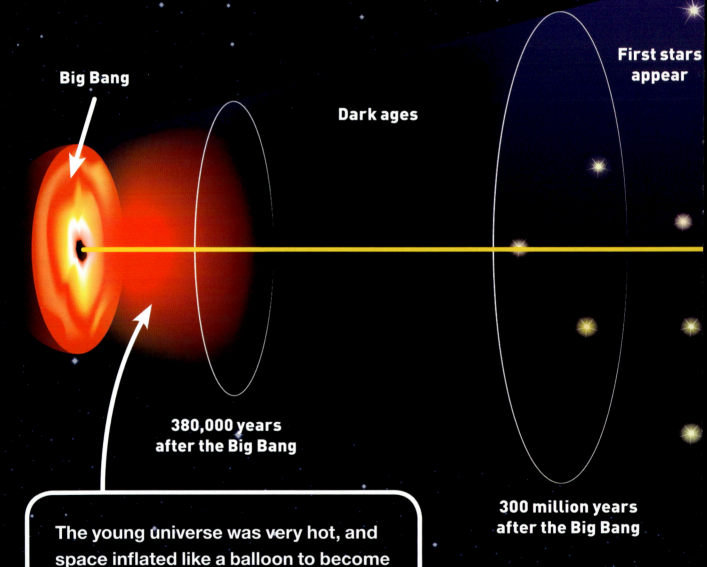

Big Bang

Dark ages

First stars appear

380,000 years after the Big Bang

300 million years after the Big Bang

The young universe was very hot, and space inflated like a balloon to become our universe. In time, it began to cool.

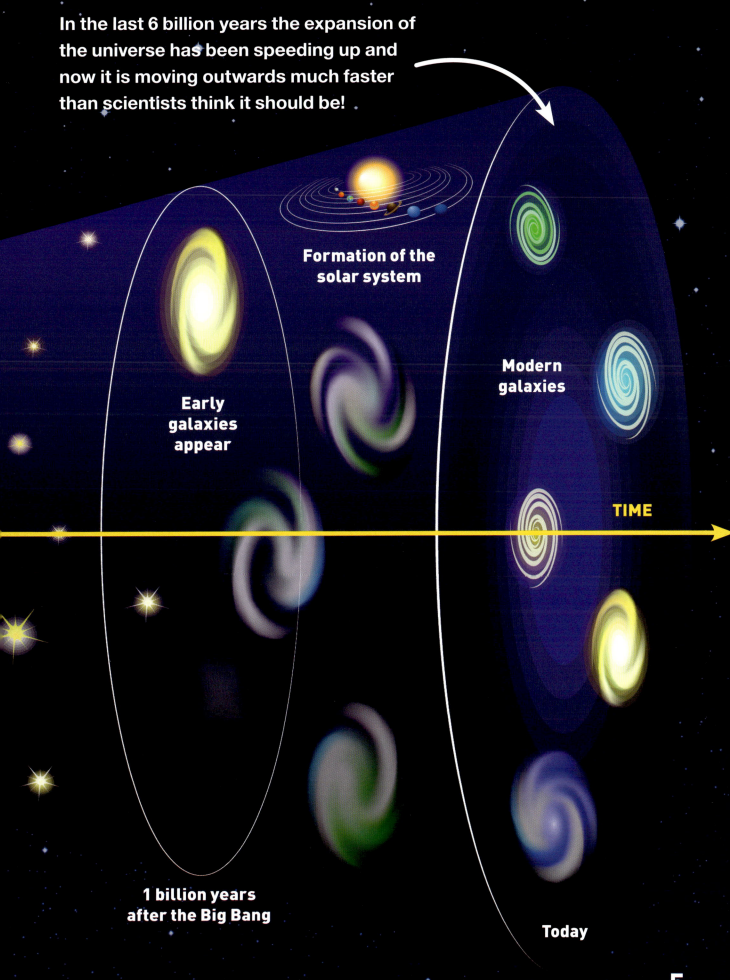

A QUIET BEGINNING

The name Big Bang is misleading: it wasn't a "big bang" at all because space is a vacuum that sound waves can't pass through. So, space is in fact quiet. The term "Big Bang" was first used on the radio by an astronomer who didn't believe in the event. He thought the universe had always existed. He was later proved wrong when scientists discovered evidence for the beginning of the universe, but the name Big Bang stuck.

AFTERGLOW

The evidence for the Big Bang was the discovery of cosmic microwaves in the universe. This is because the Big Bang created lots of energy and, over time, these energy waves stretched into long microwaves as the universe expanded. This afterglow from the Big Bang is everywhere in the universe. It is all around you! It is called Cosmic Background Radiation and is evidence that there was a moment, the Big Bang, when the universe began.

EVER-EXPANDING

Since it formed, the universe has been expanding. The thing pushing the universe apart is a mysterious force called dark energy. The space between galaxies is stretching and pushing those galaxies apart. The expansion of the universe was discovered by an astronomer named Edwin Hubble. His revelation helped scientists work out how old the universe is.

The universe continues to expand like a balloon

DID YOU KNOW?

Scientists think it would take 46 billion light-years to get to the "edge" of the universe that humans can see...with a lot of help from telescopes and technology!

SPACETIME

Before the Big Bang, there was no time and no space. Scientists, from Albert Einstein onward, discovered that space and time are actually the same thing. This is called spacetime. Spacetime may be infinite and flat—something that's very difficult for humans to imagine! The physics genius Einstein came up with two theories in the 1900s that explain spacetime. One is the theory of special relativity and the other is the theory of general relativity.

THE THEORY OF GENERAL RELATIVITY

The theory of general relativity explains gravity and states that spacetime is like a trampoline. It says that when things like planets and stars move in spacetime, they create ripples. These curves are gravity, the force that explains why things fall when you drop them.

THE THEORY OF SPECIAL RELATIVITY

The theory of special relativity says that movement is relative. The movement of one thing is always relative to the movement of another. Special relativity also explains that light always travels at the same speed: 186,000 miles (300,000 km) per second. The Theory of Special Relativity says that space and time are connected; this is spacetime. Spacetime bends around big things, such as planets and stars.

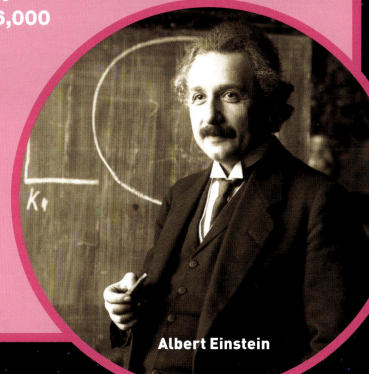
Albert Einstein

DID YOU KNOW?

The speed of light is a cosmic speed limit. It is the fastest speed possible in the universe. It is impossible for humans to travel at the speed of light. But guess what? If you could travel at the speed of light, you could go around the world 7.5 times in a second!

FORCES OF NATURE

There are four fundamental forces of nature, without which the universe would fall apart. These forces rule the way everything in the universe works. They are gravity, electromagnetism, and the strong and weak nuclear forces.

1. GRAVITY

Gravity pulls everything in the universe together. This force pulls the planets around the sun in our solar system. It pulls us down to Earth so that we don't float off into space. In supermassive black holes at the center of galaxies, gravity is superstrong. In other places in the universe, it is really weak. If you step on the moon you feel light and bounce around because gravity on the moon is weak.

DID YOU KNOW?

Gravity is the weakest of the four fundamental forces of nature.

2. WEAK NUCLEAR FORCE

Weak nuclear forces work inside atoms.

3. ELECTROMAGNETISM

Electromagnetic force is much stronger than gravity. It combines electric and magnetic forces. It is the glue holding all the atoms in the universe together.

Auroras are electromagnetic light shows

The aurora borealis seen from space

4. STRONG NUCLEAR FORCE

It is responsible for holding the nuclei of atoms together. The interaction is very strong, but has a very short range.

LIGHT IN SPACE

Light is a type of energy wave that is visible, although humans can only see a tiny part of all the energy waves that exist in the universe. We see the visible spectrum, which includes all the colors of the rainbow. There are also all sorts of rays of energy that we cannot see but that we know exist in the universe. These are: gamma rays, X-rays, ultraviolet and infrared light, microwaves, and radio waves. Each of these different energy waves are different lengths, and they travel at different speeds.

Electromagnetic spectrum

This shows the different waves of energy in order of wavelength from the longest to the shortest. All electromagnetic waves travel at the speed of light in a vacuum like space. Visible light can be seen in the middle of the spectrum.

Infrared light

Infrared light is given off by cosmic dust and stars that are warmer than the cold emptiness of space, but not hot enough to glow with light that we can see. Astronomers use special infrared cameras to find and study cooler objects in space, such as red stars, which shine in infrared.

WAVES IN SPACE

Astronomers use special kinds of telescopes and cameras to search for these different energy waves in space. They find objects in the universe that emit these energy waves and then they can learn about them.

Pleiades star cluster in infrared light

sun seen in X-rays

Ultraviolet light (UV)

Hot objects, like the sun, give off UV, a light wave that we cannot see. Luckily, our atmosphere blocks out most of these powerful rays, which can damage life on Earth. Really hot stars give off more ultraviolet light.

X-rays

X-rays have lots of energy. They are created in extreme environments like black holes, exploding stars, and crashing galaxies.

Gamma rays

These are very energetic energy waves created in the most massive star explosions of all.

UV

X-RAY

GAMMA

ENERGY

13

WILL IT ALL END?

Nobody knows how big the universe is. It may be infinite, but this idea is impossible to prove! Scientists have worked out how the universe began, but nobody knows if or how it will end.

1. BIG RIP

There could be a Big Rip in which everything in the universe is eventually torn apart...

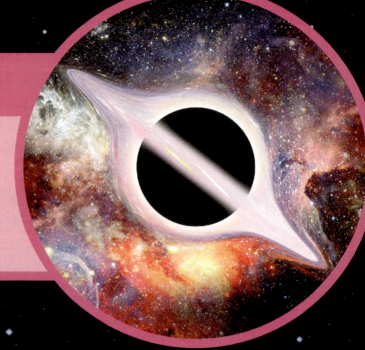

2. BIG CRUNCH

...or a Big Crunch in which the universe collapses into an immensely massive black hole.

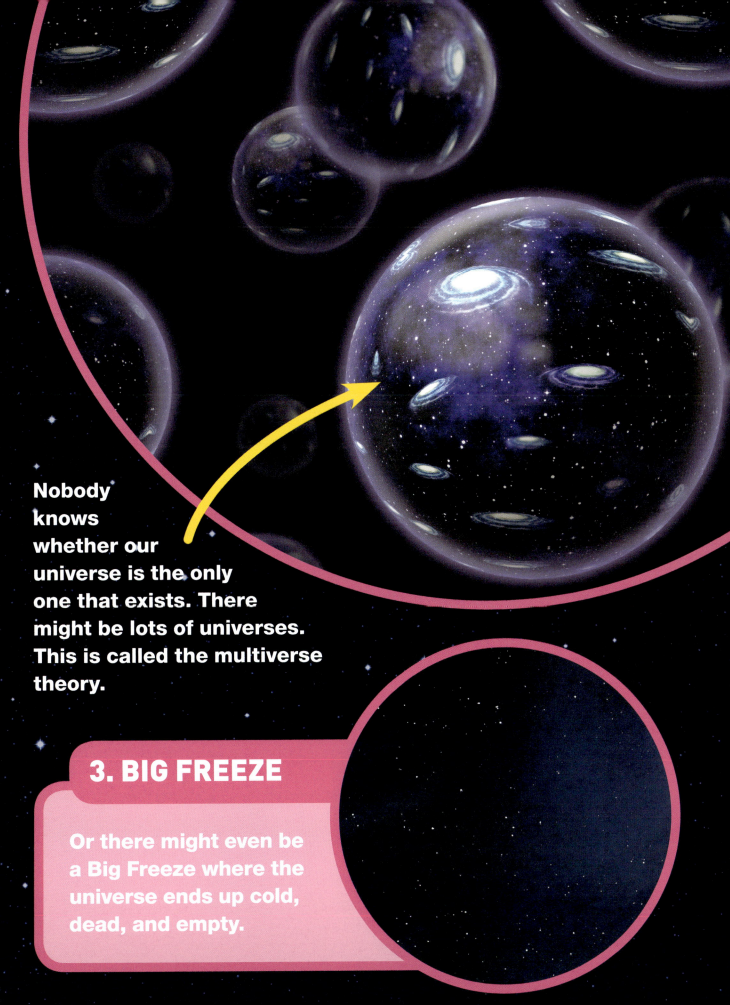

Nobody knows whether our universe is the only one that exists. There might be lots of universes. This is called the multiverse theory.

3. BIG FREEZE

Or there might even be a Big Freeze where the universe ends up cold, dead, and empty.

SCIENTISTS

OLE RØMER

(1644–1710)
This Danish astronomer was the first person to measure the speed of light. Now we know that all energy in the universe travels at the speed of light.

ALBERT EINSTEIN

(1879–1955)
A German physicist who developed two theories of relativity (see pages 8-9), which help to explain how the universe works. He explained gravity and worked out that space and time are actually the same thing. He called it spacetime.

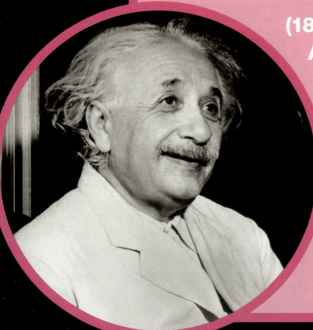

MAGGIE ADERIN-POCOCK

(1968–)
A popular space engineer, scientist, and TV presenter who enthuses children and adults alike about the wonders of the universe. She set up her own companies, which tour schools to talk about the universe. She dreamed of going into space as a child.

ROBERT WOODROW WILSON AND ARNO PENZIAS

Robert Woodrow Wilson (1936–), Arno Penzias (1933–)
These astronomers discovered Cosmic Background Radiation through the Holmdel Horn Antenna. These cosmic microwaves in the universe prove the theory of the universe beginning with the Big Bang.

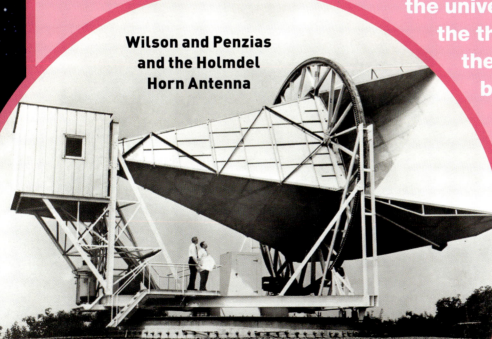

Wilson and Penzias and the Holmdel Horn Antenna

IN THE DARK

One of the biggest mysteries of space is dark energy. After the Big Bang, the universe was pushed apart by a strange, all-powerful force. This force is dark energy, and scientists think it makes up most of the universe—more than 68 percent. It is everywhere, still pushing everything in the universe apart at a faster and faster rate.

Scientists have learned about dark energy by studying the expansion of the universe and looking at how fast galaxies are moving apart. But it is one of the biggest mysteries of the cosmos because they know what it does but they don't know what it is.

A SPEEDY SURPRISE

Dark energy was discovered in the 1990s by astronomers who worked out that the expansion of the universe is accelerating rather than slowing down. This was a big surprise to space scientists. By studying exploding stars with the Hubble and other space telescopes, they found the first evidence of dark energy.

Exploding stars light research into dark energy

DARK MATTER

Dark matter is an invisible web of mysterious "stuff" that holds galaxies, and everything else in the universe, together. No one knows what it is. Scientists only really know it exists because gravity alone is not strong enough to hold galaxies together. Dark matter is pulling stars around in swirling galaxies across the universe. It is thought to make up about 27 percent of the universe.

WHY ARE THEY DARK?

We call dark energy and dark matter "dark" because we humans cannot see them. Scientists believe they exist because they help explain how scientists think the universe works. We can see other matter in the universe, such as stars, planets, and life on Earth—yet these visible objects make up only 5 percent of the universe.

WORMHOLES

No one has ever seen or found a wormhole, but scientists believe that they exist. Wormholes are believed to be like bridges across time and space in the universe or maybe portals to another universe.

TIME SHORTCUTS

Wormholes are thought to be hollow tunnels that cross from one part of the universe to another. The time taken to pass through this tunnel would be much less than it would take to travel through normal space. This means you could travel faster than the speed of light through a wormhole.

THE CHALLENGE

A wormhole would be a very dangerous place. It would probably collapse before you got a chance to travel from one end to the other.

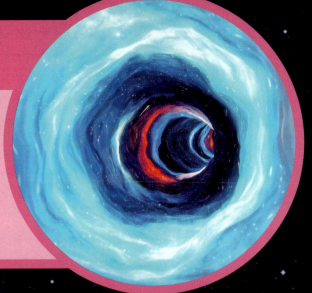

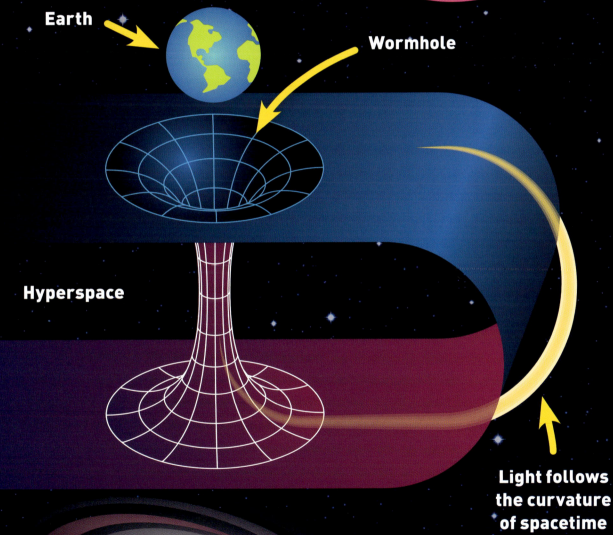

Earth

Wormhole

Hyperspace

Light follows the curvature of spacetime

Distant galaxy

LOOKING FOR LIFE

Life on our planet exists in the strangest extreme places—from frozen deserts to acidic lakes, in superheated water and in rocks deep down in the Earth. In an infinite universe, it is unlikely that life only exists on planet Earth.

DIFFERENT KINDS OF LIFE

Space scientists are looking at places where there might have been some form of life in the past, perhaps when water existed on Mars. They are also looking for evidence of tiny forms of microbial life living in extreme conditions, perhaps in the underground oceans on Jupiter's moon Europa. And they are particularly on the lookout for signs of intelligent life in interstellar space, perhaps on a distant planet in a distant solar system.

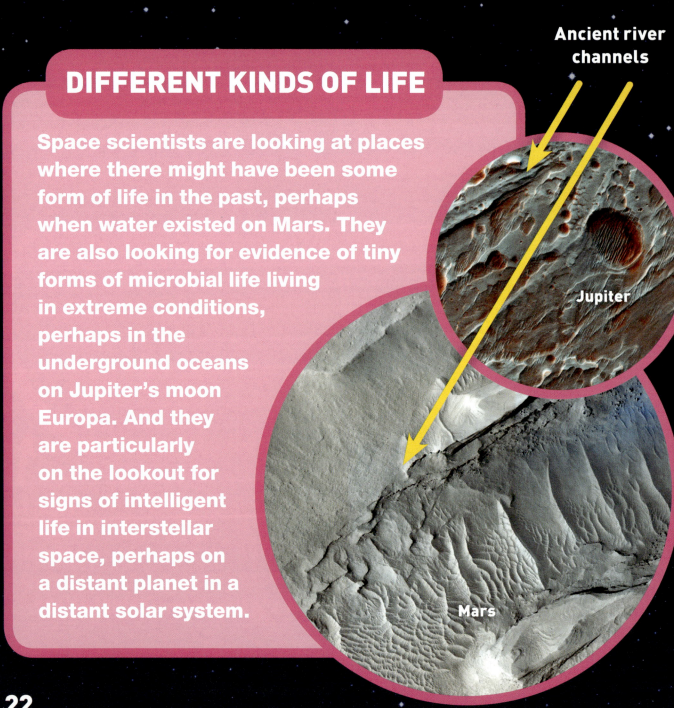

Ancient river channels

Jupiter

Mars

GOLDILOCKS ZONE

Earth orbits in the "Goldilocks zone"—just the right distance from the sun for life to be possible. Water is needed for life as we know it, and to have surface water, planets must be just the right distance from the star they are orbiting. Too close and it will evaporate; too far away and it will freeze. So, scientists are on the lookout for planets and moons orbiting in the Goldilocks zone around a star.

The Goldilocks zone where the temperature is just right

Star | Hot | Cold

DID YOU KNOW?

There is a special math equation called the Drake Equation that calculates the chances of finding other life in the universe. It turns out that there's a pretty high chance! It was worked out in 1964, but no alien life has been found since then!

FOCUS ON ALIEN LIFE

LIFE ON MARS

Scientists have been looking for signs of life on Mars for a long time. Though they have found evidence of liquid water, there are still no signs of life.

Surface of Mars

JUPITER'S MOONS

Jupiter's moon Europa has a buried ocean of liquid water.

Surface of Europa

SATURN'S MOONS

Saturn's moon Enceladus has buried oceans of water and many of the other ingredients required for life.

Enceladus

FURTHER OUT

Super-Earth exoplanet LHS 1140b is just one of the distant exoplanets in the Goldilocks zone of its faint red star. This means that it's not too hot and not too cold, so the conditions could be right for life. But this massive planet is 40 light-years away!

DID YOU KNOW?

Life on Earth probably began in deep, hot water where atoms of carbon, nitrogen, hydrogen, sulfur, and phosphorous got together. It happened at the right time in the right place, and involved a lot of luck.

ALIEN NOISES

If life is discovered elsewhere in the universe it is unlikely to look like life on Earth. It may be intelligent like us or it may be just a hot soup of bubbling bacteria. If it is intelligent, it may recognize sound. So, scientists have set up radio telescopes to act as giant ears on Earth, listening for noise signals from alien forms of life. So far there is a deafening silence from deep space.

Radio telescope

DID YOU KNOW?

Spacecraft Voyager 1 took 33 years to reach the edge of the solar system. It's now heading into interstellar space.

GOLDEN RECORD

In addition to using radio telescopes to listen from Earth, space robots carry messages from people on Earth into space with the hope that intelligent alien life will find and respond to our friendly greeting. In 1977, a golden record was sent into space on Voyager 1, which is now billions of miles from Earth in deep space.

WHAT'S ON IT?

The golden record contains 116 pictures of life on Earth, greetings from people in 55 languages, and a huge array of sounds, from whale songs to thunder, as well as music and a message from the 39th American President Jimmy Carter and the United Nations.

DISCOVERERS

VERA RUBIN

(1928–2016)
She was an astronomer famous for studying the spinning galaxies and providing evidence that most of the universe was made of dark matter.

ARTHUR C. CLARKE

(1917–2008)
He was a science fiction writer best known for writing the script and novel *2001: A Space Odyssey*. He made many popular films and became famous for his surprisingly accurate space predictions.

CARL SAGAN

(1934–1996)
He was a cosmologist and scientist famous for looking for extraterrestrial life in the universe and making astronomy popular, writing books and appearing on TV space shows.

STEPHEN HAWKING

(1942–2018)
He was an author and physicist famous for his work unraveling the mysteries of black holes and making complicated space science easier for people to understand. His book, *A Brief History of Time*, was a record-breaking best seller around the world.

GLOSSARY

alien a being from another plant

collapse to fall down or cave in

cosmic having to do with outer space or the universe

evidence something that helps show or disprove the truth of something

galaxy a large group of stars, planets, gas, and dust that form a unit within the universe

interstellar having to do with the space between stars

light-year the distance light can travel in one year

orbit to travel in a circle or oval around something, or the path used to make that trip

solar system the sun and all the space objects that orbit it, including the planets and their moons

technology using science, engineering, and other industries to invent useful tools or to solve problems. Also a machine, piece of equipment, or method created by technology.

telescope a tool that makes faraway objects look bigger and closer

theory an explanation based on facts that is generally accepted by scientists

universe everything that exists

vacuum an empty space without any matter in it

FOR MORE INFORMATION

BOOKS

Beer, Julie, and Stephanie Warren Drimmer. *Can't Get Enough Space Stuff*. Washington, DC: National Geographic, 2022.

Light, Charlie. *To the Milky Way and Beyond*: *Explorations Outside the Solar System*. Gareth Stevens Publishing, 2021.

Nargi, Lela. *Mysteries of Planets, Stars, and Galaxies*. North Mankato, MN: Capstone Press, 2021.

WEBSITES

www.planetsforkids.org/
Read more about the planets in our solar system, and other cosmic bodies, on this website.

www.ducksters.com/science/galaxies.php
Find out even more fun facts about galaxies!

Publisher's note to educators and parents: Our editors have carefully reviewed these websites to ensure that they are suitable for students. Many websites change frequently, however, and we cannot guarantee that a site's future contents will continue to meet our high standards of quality and educational value. Be advised that students should be closely supervised whenever they access the internet.

INDEX

Aderin-Pocock, Maggie 17
alien life 23, 24, 25, 26, 27, 29
Big Bang 4, 6, 8, 17, 18
black hole 10, 13, 14, 29
Clarke, Arthur C. 28
Cosmic Background Radiation 6, 17
dark energy 7, 18, 19
dark matter 19, 28
Earth 19, 20, 25, 26, 27
Einstein, Albert 8, 16
electromagnetic spectrum 12, 13
forces of nature 10, 11
Goldilocks zone 23, 25
Hawking, Stephen 29
Hubble, Edwin 7

multiverse theory 15
Penzias, Arno 17
Rømer, Ole 16
Rubin, Vera 28
Sagan, Carl 29
speed of light 9, 12, 16, 20
stars 12, 13, 18, 19, 21, 23
telescopes 7, 13, 18, 26, 27
theory of general relativity 8
theory of special relativity 9
Voyager 1 26, 27
Wilson, Robert Woodrow 17